'A Splendid College':

An Illustrated History of Teacher Training in Cheltenham, 1847-1990

DISCE UT DOCEAS

Charles

Published by Cheltenham and Gloucester
College of Higher Education 1992

The Park Campus, The Park,
Cheltenham, Gloucestershire GL50 2QF

ISBN 0 9519427 0 0

Designed by Tamasin Cole
Typeset by York House Typographic Ltd, London
Printed and bound by Cambridge University Press

Contents

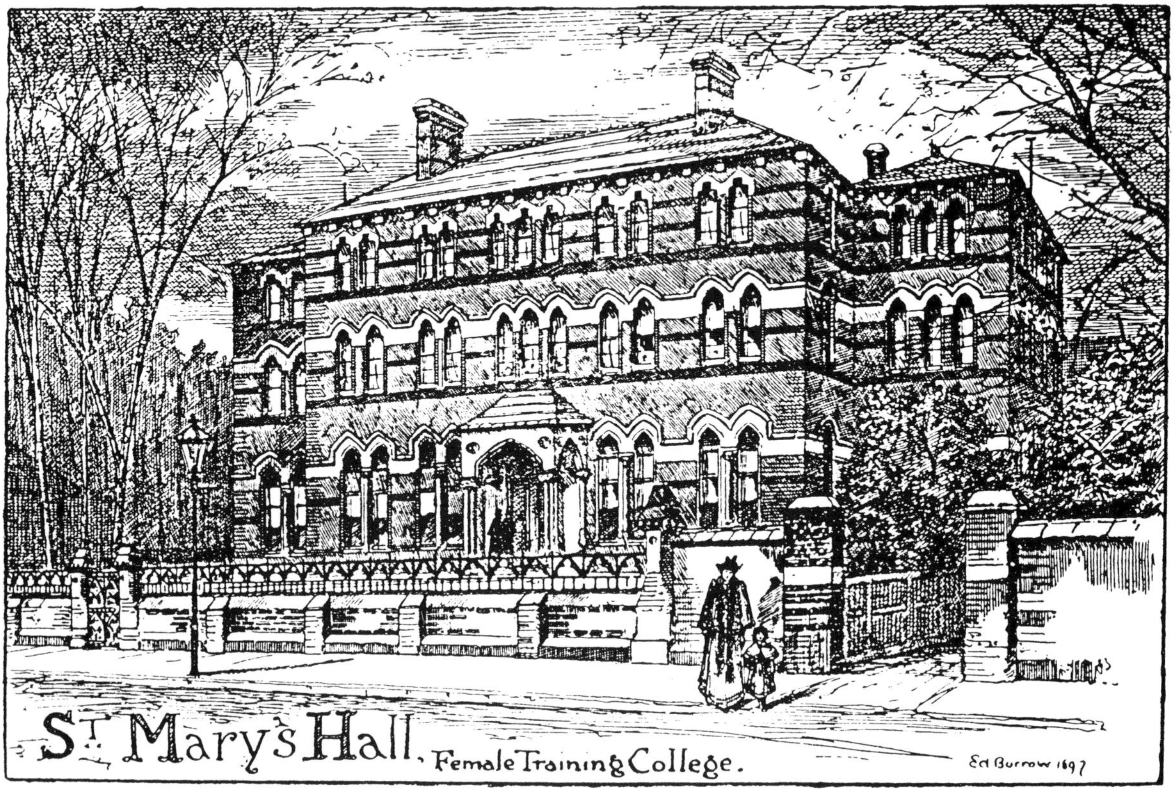

St Mary's Hall (now Shaftesbury Hall): a view of the 1890s

Preface

For over one hundred and forty years the teacher training college founded at Cheltenham in 1847 and its successor institutions have been part of the town's landscape. Their buildings are Cheltenham landmarks: the men's college, now Francis Close Hall, with its creeper-covered frontage; the women's department, now Shaftesbury Hall, looming up near the centre of the town; and since the 1930s the Fullwood or Park site to which St Mary's, by then a separate women's college, moved. Most old students and residents of Cheltenham are likely to associate these buildings either with the separate colleges of St Paul and St Mary, or else with the combined college of that name which existed from 1979 to 1990; but until 1921 the college's official name was the Training College at Cheltenham. It was one college which trained both women and men in separate departments.

The detailed history of the first hundred years of this college and its successors is contained in my book *The Training of Teachers, 1847-1947: A History of the Church Colleges at Cheltenham* (Hambledon Press, 1992). The present volume contains a brief survey of the first hundred years and continues the story up to the merger with GlosCat in 1990, out of which was formed the Cheltenham and Gloucester College of Higher Education. The first three sections give the outline history and describe the more important buildings. The next six chapters are each arranged in two parts, the first dealing with the period 1847-1947, the second with the period 1947-1990. The final three chapters are not divided. The sections of the book dealing with the first hundred years of the colleges are based on sources listed in my other book, although I have used some fresh material to vary the approach. The main sources for the later part were the annual reports, supplemented by a memoir written by Edward Bradby, by Betty Challinor's earlier book *The Story of St Mary's College* and by a number of interviews. The photographs mainly came from the college archives, although a few have been kindly lent by old members of staff. Photographs in the archives are often not dated; in these cases I have given approximate dates based on the evidence available in the photograph itself. If anyone can supply exact dates for such photographs the college would be pleased to know.

A large number of people have given me assistance in one way or another; I hope that they will forgive me if for reasons of space I do not mention them all individually. However, I would like to thank the following who have put themselves out by talking to me at length, reading drafts of the book or in some other way. They are: Jill Allport, David Ashcroft, Edward Bradby, Betty Challinor, Patti Cox, Dorothy Curtis, Dorothy Evans, Paul Harrison, Trevor Hearl, Fred Hughes, Jackie Mathis, Terry Morgan, Gordon Osborn,

John Ryan, Carol de Soissons, Janet Trotter, Margaret Webb and Helen Wright.

The research for and publication of this book and its companion were made possible by financial support from the Governors of the College of St Paul and St Mary and the Governors of the Cheltenham and Gloucester College of Higher Education. The abbreviation CPM has been used for the united College of St Paul and St Mary which existed between 1979 and 1990. The first three words of the title are taken from a letter written to her parents by Gladys Warden, a student between 1910 and 1912: 'I am sure that we all ought to feel very grateful to think we belong to such a splendid College in such a lovely town'.

Chapter 1: The First Hundred Years 1847 to 1947

Cheltenham Training College's establishment in 1847 was the result of a number of pressures and concerns which had been growing over the previous thirty years or more. The growth in population and its increasing urbanisation threatened to overwhelm such school provision as had previously existed. Concern among the governing classes centred on the potential a crowded and uneducated population might have to challenge existing authority. Teaching children to read would ensure that they could know their Bible and thus come under the influence of the Established Church or of other religious bodies. There were various solutions to the problem of finding sufficient teachers for these children, such as the

Cheltenham Training College (St Paul's) depicted in a late nineteenth-century engraving

monitorial system which relied on older children (monitors) repeating the teacher's lesson to the younger children. In the 1830s, however, continental ideas about teacher training which attached much more importance to the personal role of the teacher began to circulate in England. Acting on these ideas, various interested parties prompted the foundation from 1839 onwards of several Church of England training colleges. The colleges were supported by the National Society which also financed church schools. However, the National Society was becoming unpopular with some clergymen in the 1840s because of the increasing division within the Church of England between Evangelicals and Tractarians. Francis Close, the Evangelical incumbent of St Mary's, Cheltenham, was involved in the dispute, believing the National Society to be leaning towards Tractarianism.

Close had his own ideas on education, having helped to found a number of infant schools. These adopted what were then considered 'advanced' techniques, such as collective singing and periods of play for the children. Given his religious views and his interest in education, it is not surprising that Close welcomed an initiative by Samuel Codner, an Evangelical merchant, who had himself set up a number of schools in Newfoundland, to establish a training college in Cheltenham. From the start the college was avowedly national in its scope and aims, as opposed to most of the existing colleges which were diocesan foundations. It was probably the desire to establish a national reputation which led to the appointment of no less than two hundred governors, one hundred clerical and one hundred

Francis Close (reproduced by permission of Cheltenham Art Gallery and Museum)

lay, from all parts of the country. Governors at that time made a financial contribution (a guinea per annum if lay, half a guinea if clerical), recommended students to the college and sometimes employed them as teachers afterwards. In practice the large number of governors meant that the connection of many of them with the college was somewhat tenuous. The effective work of the governors was carried out by a small executive committee, overseen by a largely ceremonial general committee.

The college at first operated in rented accommodation. However, the government was at that time giving a generous building grant which helped to pay for the construction of a building housing up to one hundred men, as well as houses for a principal and vice-principal. Opened in 1850, this was the core of what we now know as Francis Close Hall. The women had to put up with rented accommodation for another twenty years. According to Close, the decision to build the men's college first was taken because the demand for male teachers outstripped the demand for female; but throughout the nineteenth century the men were given precedence when it came to expenditure.

The home of the women's department from 1850 to 1869 was the old hospital, renamed St Mary's Hall after the original parish church of Cheltenham. Government building grants having ceased, it was only the closure of

Highbury, an Evangelical college in London, which released enough money for a permanent St Mary's Hall to be built (now Shaftesbury Hall). There is no record of a separate name for the men's department until the 1880s, by which time the student's were calling it St Paul's after their parish church.

By the 1860s numbers in the men's department had settled at about ninety, and at St Mary's Hall at about sixty. With a few fluctuations they stayed at that level until the 1890s. Cheltenham was for a time the largest training college, and even its individual departments (which ran more or less independently under the one principal) were larger than many individual colleges. So what seems a small institution now should be set in the perspective of the time. In other ways it and the other colleges quickly established a very similar routine. The training period ran for two years. Hours were long – typically thirty hours of lectures per week with additional supervised preparation. Under the influence of the inspectorate, the more academic subjects tended to be squeezed out of the syllabus in favour of plenty of basic maths and grammar. Teaching practice usually took place in practising schools attached to the institution. Recreation was very limited, although for the men opportunities did increase steadily through the nineteenth century. Most students were called 'Queen's Scholars' and paid for by the government, although financial cutbacks in the 1860s led to the imposition of a small fee. Students would have started as pupil teachers in elementary schools, learning and teaching at the same time. Most went to college at eighteen or nineteen, although there were always a few older students, especially among the men.

Charles Bromby as Bishop of Tasmania

Cheltenham was different in some aspects. Its Evangelical foundation expressed itself in the insistence that students worship in the local, Evangelical, parish churches. The vigorous first principal, C H Bromby, later Bishop of Tasmania, had encouraged a degree of self-government, at least among the men students. His successor from 1864, Robert Chamney, although a kindly man and popular among the students, was not dynamic; as a result the conservative instincts of the governors held sway, and the college stood still for almost thirty years. It still retained a good reputation, St Mary's Hall being considered one of the leading women's colleges (strictly speaking it was a department of the main college). St Mary's benefited after 1869 from its new building and also from the leadership of Isabella Reynolds, 'Lady Superintendent' from 1864 to 1886, who was very highly thought of by the inspectorate. She supervised both the academic and domestic sides. She left to become Chamney's third wife, but died before him to leave him thrice a widower.

Before Chamney's death in office in 1894, at the age of seventy-three, change was already underway. The elementary school curriculum was being broadened from its original concentration on the three 'R's (and for girls, needlework); new ideas which envisaged the classroom as a brighter and more creative place were coming in, particularly at infant and lower junior level; and, at the other end of the age range, a big increase in secondary education was under way, with a particular emphasis on scientific and technical work. At the same time forward-looking inspectors and officials at the Education Department (from 1900 the Board of Education) pressed the training colleges to modernise. Chamney and the then governors made a few changes, but real change only began with the appointment of Henry Bren as principal in 1895. Bren had been principal of a school in India and then secretary to the Church Missionary Society. He was a

Henry Bren

physically imposing man, whom the students seem to have found somewhat aloof. His influence on the college was fundamental. With demand for places buoyant, and with the governors by now supportive of change, Bren ploughed the small financial surplus made every year back into expansion. By the early 1900s St Paul's and St Mary's Hall both took 120 students. At the same time Bren was building or enlarging student common rooms, laboratories and other buildings. By the 1900s the college was recognised as the best for science in the country, turning out dozens of students every year – mainly men but some women – with London University intermediate awards ('inters'). A few students took full degrees and all, of course, continued to take the teaching certificate. In spite of this, teaching hours were cut and private study encouraged. Recreational and sporting opportunities increased although student life remained highly regulated.

Bren's greatest coup was to buy, in 1903-4, a large house on the London Road, The Priory, and turn it into a hostel for women students. By this time teaching had become established as a good career for women, offering them relatively high salaries, so demand for places was strong. The Priory was open to nonconformists, thus heading off a threat from Gloucestershire County Council to set up one of the new LEA colleges and break the local denominational monopoly on teacher training. Bren increased female student numbers to 200 and made the college once again the largest in the country. Finally, he added the crowning glory of the chapel, opened in 1910.

While the 1890s and 1900s had seen buoyancy and expansion, the aftermath of the First World War was to see stagnation. The government limited student numbers. It also forced the division into separate colleges of

The entrance front of St Paul's

the men's and women's departments, carried out in 1921. The colleges were run as separate entities, retaining one governing body. The division was the result of a laudable policy to increase the number of female lecturers, and to give women the opportunity to reach positions of authority as principals. For Cheltenham, however, it posed difficult problems since the finances of the two departments were intermingled, while a number of the male staff also taught female students. On its own, St Paul's would only have had 120 students and would hardly have been viable. The issues were thrashed out through the 1920s: St Mary's gave up thirty student places to St Paul's, while more women staff were appointed and the older male staff gradually retired.

Anna Monk, the first principal of St Mary's, worked tirelessly to move the residential places out of the by now aging St Mary's Hall. As at St Paul's, all the students slept in dormitories, divided into cubicles, and had no private study facilities. These arrangements, which in the nineteenth century were standard practice, were increasingly unacceptable. The Fullwood site was acquired by St Mary's in 1931 with funds from the winding up of the Home and Colonial College, the first Evangelical (although not specifically Anglican) college, founded in 1836. The Fullwood hostel was finally started in 1938, the year Anna Monk retired to be succeeded by the dynamic Winifred Jones. Fullwood was designed to house all the students from St Mary's Hall and The Priory, being built with the help of a large loan from the Church of England's Central Board of Finance. From the First World War the church had taken an increasing interest in its colleges, although it was held back by lack of money.

St Paul's continued to maintain a sound reputation under its principal Wilfred Beck, but it too suffered from financial stringency. Science, for instance, once the leading subject in the college's academic curriculum, was allowed to run down; student reminiscences of the 1940s speak of the laboratories remaining almost unchanged from their state as revealed by pre-1914 photographs. Although in 1928 the college had joined with others in the Western Joint Board for examinations, run by the University of Bristol for a number of colleges, academic standards do not seem to have risen. They may even have fallen, as the work for the London University external examinations faded away in the 1920s.

The aftermath of the Second World War helped to bring about major changes. Expansion became the rule: the school-leaving age was raised to fifteen in 1947; that and an increased birth-rate produced a big increase in the demand for teachers. In the same year, the two Cheltenham colleges and others became formally linked with Bristol University by becoming participants in its Institute of Education. The year 1947, the two colleges' centenary, was a momentous year for them in other ways as well.

Chapter 2: From Centenary to Merger 1947 to 1990

The post-war years were to bring both challenges and problems to the twin colleges. The challenges included the increasing number of students, changing academic requirements, and the growing demands placed on all church colleges by the outside world. The problems included the inadequacies of many of the college buildings; St Paul's in particular had been little altered for the last forty years.

Wilfred Beck

In 1949, before the main changes began, Wilfred Beck retired to become Dean of Worcester Cathedral. He was replaced by Edward Bradby who had been Principal of Royal College, Colombo, Ceylon, and subsequently of Eastbourne Emergency Training College (emergency training colleges provided shortened courses for ex-servicemen). Beck was the last principal to combine the role with that of chaplain. From 1949 a separate chaplain was appointed. Initially he was shared by both colleges but in 1961, with the opening of the chapel at The Park, St Mary's had its own chaplain; with the 1979 merger the college chaplaincy was united again. Also in 1949 the college's foundation document, virtually unaltered since 1848, was amended to bring it up to date. The old-fashioned title 'Training School Association' was altered to 'Cheltenham Training Colleges Association'; and the so-called general committee of the governors of the association, which had never been very active, was replaced by a council. This contained members from outside bodies such as Bristol University and the LEA. In 1979 a further alteration in connection with the merger was to substitute the term 'fellow' for 'life governor', as the one hundred clerical and one hundred lay members of the association had been called since its foundation. The council members then became the only individuals with the title of governor.

In the immediate post-war years St Mary's, where Winifred Jones remained as principal until 1960, had around 250 students. The great majority of St Mary's students still lived in residence, either at Fullwood or in one of the hostels, Broadlands, Benton, Ireton, Pallas and Dunholme, all of which were bought during or just after the war. At St Paul's, the two hundred or so students lived either in college or at The Priory, where Reg Riley was warden. The pressure to expand led St Paul's to consider building on a completely new site, thus giving rise to a little-known and highly profitable transaction. In 1946 the college had alarmed the town council by suggesting that St Paul's might move from Cheltenham if it did not have room to expand. A site of 130 acres was available at Benhall, near the present location of GCHQ. The council persuaded the owners of the land to sell to the college by holding out the possibility of a compulsory purchase order. Inability to finance building on the site led to the scheme being indefinitely shelved; in 1955 the land was sold to Wimpey's for housing with the college clearing a profit of £50,000. The profit was equivalent to a million pounds or more at 1992 prices. Taking a very long view, it would have been an ideal site for the present institution; but no one could have been expected to anticipate that far ahead.

Instead of expanding at Benhall, the college bought Rosehill, near the racecourse. Its gardens could be used for the rural science course while the old gardens at The Folley could be used to enlarge the playing fields. The extra accommodation Rosehill made available allowed the much-needed modernisation of St Paul's original buildings to go ahead between 1952 and 1956. The dormitories and cubicles, which must have been among the last in the country to survive, were converted into study bedrooms with wash-basins – an advance over Fullwood, where communal washing remained in force until the late 1980s. Very soon after this, in 1958, the colleges were among those chosen to expand their training places to 400 each. The unexpectedly high birth rate and the long-standing plan to lengthen the training period to three years lay behind the increase. To support it the Ministry of Education increased its building grant from 50 per cent to 75 per cent. The decision was taken to expand St Mary's at Fullwood, or the Park site as it came to be called. Up to that time Fullwood had been purely residential, with academic work taking place in the old St Mary's Hall. The new plan called for the concentration of academic work at the Park, and to that effect a range of new buildings was constructed. When the new buildings were finished in 1961 the original St Mary's Hall building was transferred to St Paul's' ownership and renamed Shaftesbury Hall. The plan was neat and logical but it left St Paul's with a number of scattered sites and elderly buildings.

The changes in the size and physical structure of the colleges were matched by the changes in academic courses. For the majority of students the first big change was the shift from examination to continuous assessment, consequent upon adoption of the new Bristol Institute Certificate courses from 1947-48 onwards. (Examinations were reinstated for the BEd degree in the 1960s; as degree work spread they again became a major method of assessment.) From the late 1940s a limited number of third-year students in each college specialised in certain subjects where there was a shortage of highly trained teachers, such as PE at St Paul's and needlework, art and design at St Mary's. In 1960, after years of preparation, three years of training became standard for all new entrants. Fittingly this advance coincided with Winifred Jones' retirement after twenty-two years as Principal of St Mary's. During her time the college had endured the vicissitudes of the war years, moved to Fullwood, and doubled its numbers. She was replaced by Valentine Hall, previously Principal of Ripon Training College and, like Winifred Jones, an educational psychologist.

Winifred Jones and Berry

The rapid expansion of the late 1950s continued into the 1960s as projections of the number of schoolchildren were constantly increased. The original target of 400 students for each college was soon outdated and by the end of the decade the colleges had around 700 students apiece. The increased numbers were accommodated partly in new halls of residence, at Rosehill and New Hall (later renamed Challinor Hall) at the Park. Other building developments were the Hardwick teaching block for St Paul's, named after an old student, and in 1974 the swimming pool built on the same site with financial help, like many college improvements, from old students. The much larger numbers of students involved a massive increase in the use of lodgings, while other students shared flats. The new arrangements formed a major departure from the hitherto tightly-knit community ethos of each college, although significant elements of this remained.

Academically the 1960s was to see a further change, building on the groundwork of the three-year course. This was the introduction of the four-year BEd course, which produced its first graduates in 1969. BEd students followed the three-year certificate course, still that taken by the majority in the 1960s, and then pursued their special subject and the theory of education in more depth in the fourth year. In order to support this, the colleges technically became schools of education affiliated to the University of Bristol; they also, in 1966, set up their own academic boards. In something of a contrast with present-day practice, all academic staff at St Paul's were board members; at St Mary's about one third were, although all staff belonged to an academic council which submitted proposals to the board.

The period from the late 1940s to the late 1960s had seen a transformation in the two colleges. Numbers had increased from around 450 students to around 1,400. Contacts with the outside world had increased. Academically, the colleges aimed higher, an aim which the Bristol University Institute of Education did much to help them fulfil. Academic development in which the staff were fully involved had become an integral part of the colleges' work.

The Park in the early 1970s

Although it is misleading to portray the two colleges' history as neatly compartmentalised into decade-long periods, it is true that each decade had a particular leitmotif. That of the 1960s was optimism and expansion; that of the 1970s contraction and a degree of pessimism about the future of all smaller colleges. Before the clouds gathered Valentine Hall retired from St Mary's in 1970 and Edward Bradby from St Paul's in 1972. Miss Hall was replaced by Gwen Owen, formerly Vice-Principal of St Martin's, Lancaster; Mr Bradby by Guy Barnes, formerly Vice-Principal of King Alfred's, Winchester, after an interim term during which John Priestley, the Vice-Principal of St Paul's, took over the reins. By now the James Report had been published. This foreshadowed a fall in the number of trainee teachers and was followed by a White Paper giving target figures for trainee teachers amounting to about half the existing number of places. The next few years were difficult ones in which the combined number in the two colleges fell to around 1,200. But the reputation of both colleges – St Mary's, for instance, was usually ranked third among women's colleges – helped them to survive and suffer smaller reductions than other colleges; their role as the only colleges with an Anglican Evangelical commitment was also important. In spite of the difficulties of those years the achievements of the two colleges, which by now worked closely together on academic development, were considerable.

One result of the James Report and its aftermath was a reduction in university involvement with the Cheltenham colleges. As with a number of other colleges the Council for National Academic Awards (CNAA) took over validation, first of the BEd and later of other degrees. An important exception was Post-Graduate Certificate of Education work, started in a number of subjects in 1972, which continued to be validated by Bristol. There is less of such work now than there once was, but there is still an important primary training course. The BEd was revalidated by CNAA in 1975, and within a few years the certificate course faded away. Of equal significance in the long run was to be the validation of the BSc in geography and geology in 1977, the two colleges' first diversified degree. This was followed in 1980 by the BA in Combined Studies, encompassing humanities subjects. As part of this diversification the colleges strengthened the provision they already made for overseas students, providing courses for Rhodesian and later Nigerian students.

The upheaval in the world of the colleges had been accompanied by numerous mergers. The students' unions of both Cheltenham colleges had supported the colleges' merger since the early 1970s and in the mid 70s the BEd degree was planned jointly between the two colleges and the Gloucestershire College of Education. It was intended to be the first stage of co-operation leading eventually to a merger with that and other colleges to form a so-called Gloucestershire Institute of Education. In the event the Gloucester College of Education (housed in what is now the Oxtalls site of the present college) closed, while legal and financial difficulties bedevilled the proposed institute. It led a shadowy existence until it was wound up in 1979. However, the proposed merger between St Mary's and St Paul's grew in impetus. Union was achieved in 1979, with Guy Barnes as the Principal of the new College of St Paul and St Mary (CPM). John Priestley again took over the principalship of St Paul's in the last two terms of its independent existence while Guy Barnes prepared the organisation of the new college; Gwen Owen retired in the summer of 1979. A new name was required for what had been the main site of St Paul's. It became Francis Close Hall, after the effective founder of the original institution.

The themes of the 1970s were continued into the 1980s, although gradually government policy turned from contraction to re-expansion. The BEd course had already developed an honours route. After revalidation in 1982, it became a four-year honours course. The BSc and BA degrees also advanced to honours in the early 1980s. To provide a suitable academic environment for honours degree work a research committee was set up. Research was fostered by this and in other ways, providing support for a variety of post-graduate degrees. Notable steps were the MEd starting in 1983, supervision of doctoral study, and MAs in Cultural Studies and in Church, Religion and Society which were validated just before the 1990 merger, recruiting their first students in September of that year.

Another important development of the 1980s was the growth in the number of mature students taking degrees. It was not new for the college to take such students. After the Second World War many male students were ex-servicemen. St Paul's continued to take a fair number of mature students; St Mary's took fewer until the mid 1960s, when a special two-year certificate course was laid on for such students. By the late 1970s in-service training for teachers was an important part of the college's total provision, including a Bristol University validated BEd taken part time by many serving teachers; in addition many of the overseas students were mature. It was in the 1980s, however, that the number of mature students on the main CNAA degrees expanded rapidly, facilitated by the introduction of part-time routes, first for the BA and then the BSc. These and other efforts in the 1980s to widen the college's basis of recruitment symbolise its commitment to enhance opportunities for all groups in society to experience higher education.

From 1986, the date of Guy Barnes' retirement and of the appointment of Janet Trotter as principal, it became increasingly clear that government policy favoured the growth of larger institutions. Taken together with changes in funding resulting from the passing of the 1988 Education Act, this raised doubts about the future of GlosCat, the combined higher and further education institution run by Gloucestershire County Council. It was decided to disaggregate GlosCat into further and higher education sections, the latter to merge with St Paul and St Mary to form the new Cheltenham and Gloucester College of Higher Education. The new institution combined GlosCat's strengths in fine art, fashion, landscape architecture, business studies and hotel management with St Paul and St Mary's strengths in teacher education, the humanities, geography and geology. The new college was formed on 1 April 1990. Through rapid growth, and by gaining the right to accredit its own degrees, the college hopes to achieve university status in the near future.

Chapter 3: Buildings

The original college buildings, now Francis Close Hall, were designed by Samuel Daukes. Daukes was an established Cheltenham architect. He owned the Park, an odd coincidence given its future importance in college affairs. His commissions included Cheltenham Station, a sad shadow of its former self after the removal of his Doric portico. Daukes also designed Cirencester Agricultural College and the Middlesex Lunatic Asylum at Colney Hatch. Daukes was quite happy to design in whatever style seemed appropriate. In the language of the time, he was an eclectic architect. For the college he produced a picturesque Gothic ensemble with a low, elongated frontage – one of his trademarks. The original building had cloisters on the north side of the quadrangle; due to subsequent infilling, including the building over of the cloisters, the quadrangle is now smaller than the original. Much of the building was not for students' use, but was taken up by the principal's house (on the left of the frontage viewed from the south), the vice-principal's (on the right), and the superintendent master's (on the north-east corner next to the dining hall).

An aerial view of St Paul's

St Paul's: the tower and the quadrangle in the 1950s

The first additions were the practising schools, built by the young George Frederick Bodley in 1854. Bodley was to become one of Britain's leading church architects, his career spanning the second half of the nineteenth century. The practising schools were probably his first building, so their importance is considerable. Bodley was a convinced Gothicist, and this conviction shows in his work. Bodley was also a brother-in-law of Bromby, as was the first vice-principal, Thomas Bodley. G F Bodley's commission must have owed itself to this connection rather than to his religious views, because he was a high churchman. Later, when Bromby became Bishop of Tasmania, Bodley received the commission for his cathedral, St David's.

From the 1890s on there were numerous additions to St Paul's, as the men's department was known by then, as numbers and facilities expanded. Particularly notable were the criticism room and laboratory block of 1902, and the gymnasium/assembly hall of 1907. This was burned down in 1914

The old assembly hall after the 1914 fire

and the present building (across the lawn from the chapel) put up in its place. Suggestions have been made from time to time that militant suffragettes were responsible for the fire, although the police never allocated responsibility. The chapel itself, by Hodgson Fowler, was built in 1909-10. It is sensitive to the other college buildings and in the view of David Verey (the author of the Gloucestershire *Buildings of England*) the whole complex contains the best examples of nineteenth- and twentieth-century Gothic in Cheltenham. The result of all this building was that the college as a whole was regarded as the best equipped of all church training colleges by the First World War. For the next forty years little was done, and by the 1950s major internal rebuilding became essential: it was carried out to designs by the Cheltenham architects Thomas Overbury and Son.

The acquisition of Rosehill gave St Paul's another building of some architectural note. Built around 1824, and possibly designed by J B Papworth, an early nineteenth-century architect who also had a hand in the building of the Landsdown area, it was one of Cheltenham's large private houses until eventually becoming a hotel. Subsequent to its purchase by the college, a number of modern buildings providing extra residential accommodation were added. Worth noting also is St Paul's House, a late nineteenth-century building opposite St Paul's church, which was a centre for the training of mature and overseas students in the late 1960s and 1970s. This returns us to Francis Close Hall, as it now is. Increasingly neglected over the last ten years for lack of funds, it is good to know that it will again play a vital part in the new institution in the 1990s and beyond.

After two-and-a-half years in Monson Villa, a large rented house, the 'female department' moved to the old hospital in the lower High Street and took the name St Mary's Hall. A handsome building, constructed in about 1834, it has been well-restored recently as Normandy House after many years of neglect. It is a curious fact that the landlord while the college was in occupation was the Great Western Railway. This was the legacy of a scheme to build a direct line from Oxford to Gloucester through Cheltenham (Daukes was to have designed the station). Regular travellers by train from Cheltenham to London will regret that the line was never built.

Elegant though the old hospital looked, it was cramped and inconvenient. The new St Mary's Hall of 1869 provided good accommodation for the time in the sombre building which is now called Shaftesbury Hall. It was built on the site of a farm – a testimony to how in those days country and town still intermingled – and was designed by J T Darby, a local architect. In the late nineteenth and early twentieth centuries there were many additions and extensions, including the purchase of the Quaker Meeting House of 1835, part of which was later used as a laboratory. The site and buildings passed from St Mary's to St Paul's in 1961,when the main building was renamed. The Earl of Shaftesbury had been the college's first president but since he never played any active part in college affairs the new name was somewhat factitious. More notable architecturally than St Mary's Hall was The Priory, which was a large early nineteenth-century house (Wellington stayed there in 1828) with a giant Corinthian order. It passed to St Paul's after the war, and the college vacated it in 1959. It was 'stupidly demolished', in David Verey's words, in 1968.

The Park laid out as a zoo

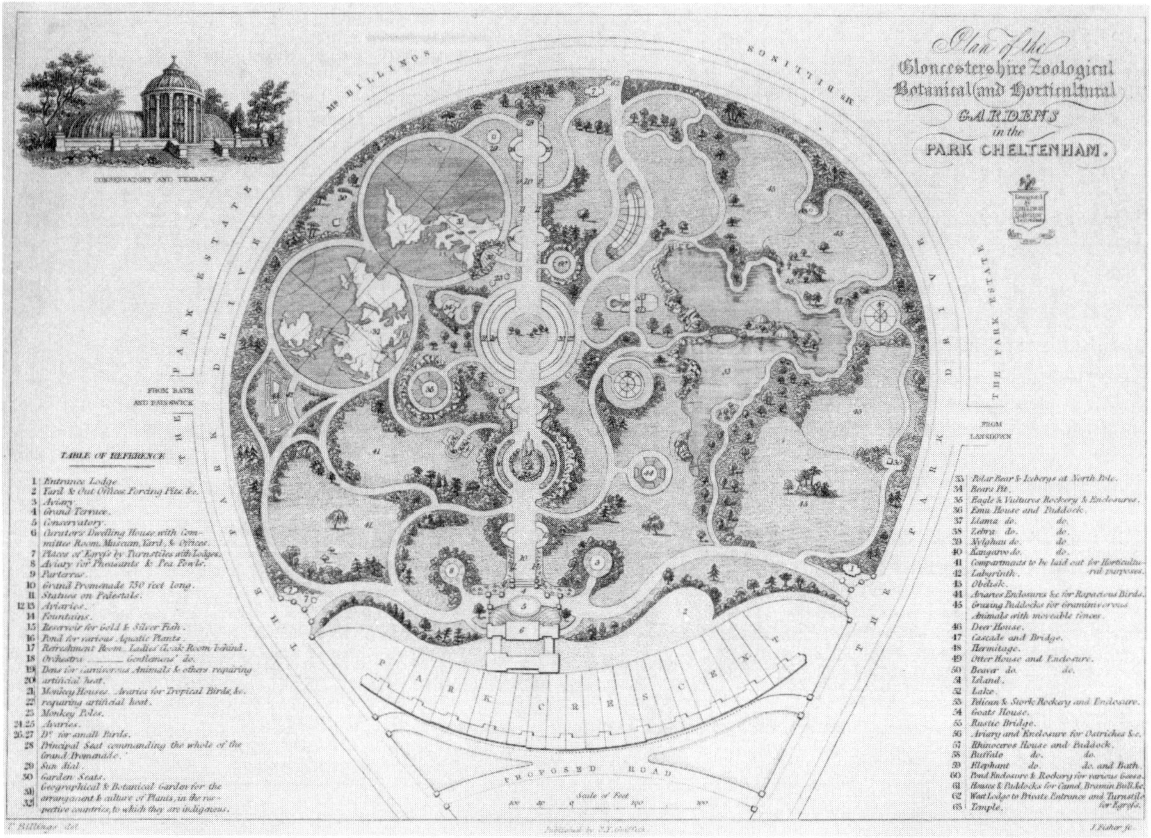

Fullwood under construction in 1939

The acquisition of Fullwood was to bring other buildings of architectural interest to the college. The Park, of which Fullwood was the main house, was enclosed by an oval tree-lined carriage drive, and for a short time was laid out as a zoo. The zoo failed and the estate was subsequently bought by Daukes. The large houses which surround the Park, some of which are now owned by the college, were mainly built in the 1840s. Daukes himself may have designed the Italianate Cornerways, latterly the stronghold of the English department. The original Fullwood House, to which most of the land of the Park was attached, was built in 1847, although the conservatory was added by a later owner, Mrs MacKnight Crawford. By the 1920s the estate was owned by Ursuline nuns, who ran a small school there. The Fullwood residential block, built between 1939 and 1940, is at first sight an incongruous addition to the stucco villas with their low-pitched roofs. But maybe a complete contrast rather than an attempt to blend in was the best solution. The detailing is quite good and Fullwood is certainly solidly built.

In this it is something of a contrast to the college's post-war buildings. The bulk of these, the main classroom block (now mainly administration offices and the library) together with the assembly hall and gym were built between 1958 and 1961; the old assembly hall then became known as Derwent Hall and a small chapel was added. Later additions include the students' union (1969), built partly with money given by the students themselves; and the primary centre, opened by HRH Princess Royal in 1987. Cheerful enough in appearance, several of these buildings suffer from the ills of modern construction, namely excessive heat in summer and water leakage. Nevertheless the site remains a fine one and, in spite of all the building, the lake end of the Park can still seem delightfully secluded.

The Priory in St Mary's days

Chapter 4: Everyday Life

Until the 1890s, the college year started in January and lasted around forty weeks. There were two terms only, with vacations over Christmas and the New Year and in the summer; the men and women started and finished their terms at different times to avoid the dangers of contact at the railway station. Their segregation was total except for joint choral singing under strict surveillance. Segregation was easy to enforce because the women, in particular, were regimented. They were only allowed out on 'class walks' under the control of senior students known as monitresses. For the rest of the time their life was a round of study, with time for some music or reading only in the evenings, late on Saturday afternoons and on Sundays – when there were also two church services a day. The men had more responsibility for their own discipline and a little more free time, in particular Saturday afternoon which they used for games. From 1881 a popular activity was amateur soldiering with the college volunteer company (the volunteers were Victorian precursors of the territorials).

In the 1890s the college year changed to the more familiar September-July format, with three terms of about twelve weeks each. The period around the turn of the century was to see other changes in everyday routine. Both women and men now had a lighter timetable, with free time in the early afternoon. Women could go out shopping in twos, while both sexes had more time for sport and hobbies. Also in this period, the men developed initiation rites and informal ways by which the seniors 'discip-

A rare photograph of an initiation rite, possibly 1929

lined' the juniors. These occurred in other training colleges as well. In some ways they strengthened the *esprit de corps* which already existed, but they also involved a degree of brutality which made many students detest them. New students were subjected to a mock exam (sample question: 'What do you know of the educational value of Tiddley-Winks and Marbles. Which do you prefer and why?'). Later they were forcibly plunged into a bath containing various revolting substances such as horse dung. This took place outside in November. Further pressure was kept up by the Jury, a group of students dressed up in tailcoats and top hats who subjected juniors to various forms of harassment. For instance, juniors had to use one side of the stairs in the front porch; anyone using the seniors' side was liable to get a cold bath from the Jury. A gentler side to life in St Paul's was represented by the Bishop, a senior student who ministered to minor injuries. He also led the Bishop's choir, four students who, once a fortnight on a Sunday evening, padded silently around the dormitories, stopping to sing hymns and anthems. Students' reminiscences often mention the sound of the choir as one of the best memories of their college career.

Most St Mary's students, or Sims as they were called, seem to have been very happy at the college in the slightly more relaxed atmosphere of the twentieth century, while still having little time for much but work. Nevertheless there was a widening of recreational activities. In the 1900s there were expeditions mounted by the Archaeological and Cycling Societies, morris-dancing, a magazine and plays. By the inter-war years women students increasingly chafed at the prohibition on their talking to St Paul's students or meeting them in any way except through membership of the choir. One student wrote of the early 1920s 'of course many of the girls

Friends at St Mary's Hall, 1912

corresponded with the "Paulites" and some of the braver ones would meet'. By the end of the 1930s this prohibition had been lifted as had others such as the insistence on wearing hats in public; inter-college dances began at this time.

When training colleges were first built, it was taken for granted that the students would sleep in dormitories with cubicles, and work and study in classrooms. Although St Mary's students managed to decorate their cubicles, the system gave little privacy and became increasingly outdated. It was also a major fire risk, with the huge open spaces of the dormitories and the wooden partitions of the cubicles. Nevertheless it was not until the building of Fullwood that the system began to be abandoned. Some of the informal social life at St Mary's revolved around the dormitories. Gladys Warden, at The Priory just before the First World War, recorded in a letter home that the girls in the dormitory below had held a 'dorm supper' as three birthdays fell in the one week. The authorities agreed, and the girls 'provided their own tuck and borrowed plates, spoons, etc.' For the men, classrooms were the venue for friendly rivalry. For instance, Troy and Nineveh, as the junior classrooms were called in the nineteenth century, had an annual rugby match.

Although the diet was always spartan, it was reasonably substantial in quantity. In June 1880, for instance, the men each consumed around 27lb of meat (presumably this included waste), 10 loaves of bread, and 20 pints of beer. The women ate considerably less: about 13lb of meat and 6 loaves of bread each in the month. They made up somewhat on biscuits, which the men did not have at all (1lb each) and milk (10 pints). The women also had beer, although only about 8 pints each. Beer-drinking reduced the need to

A dormitory at The Priory in the Edwardian period

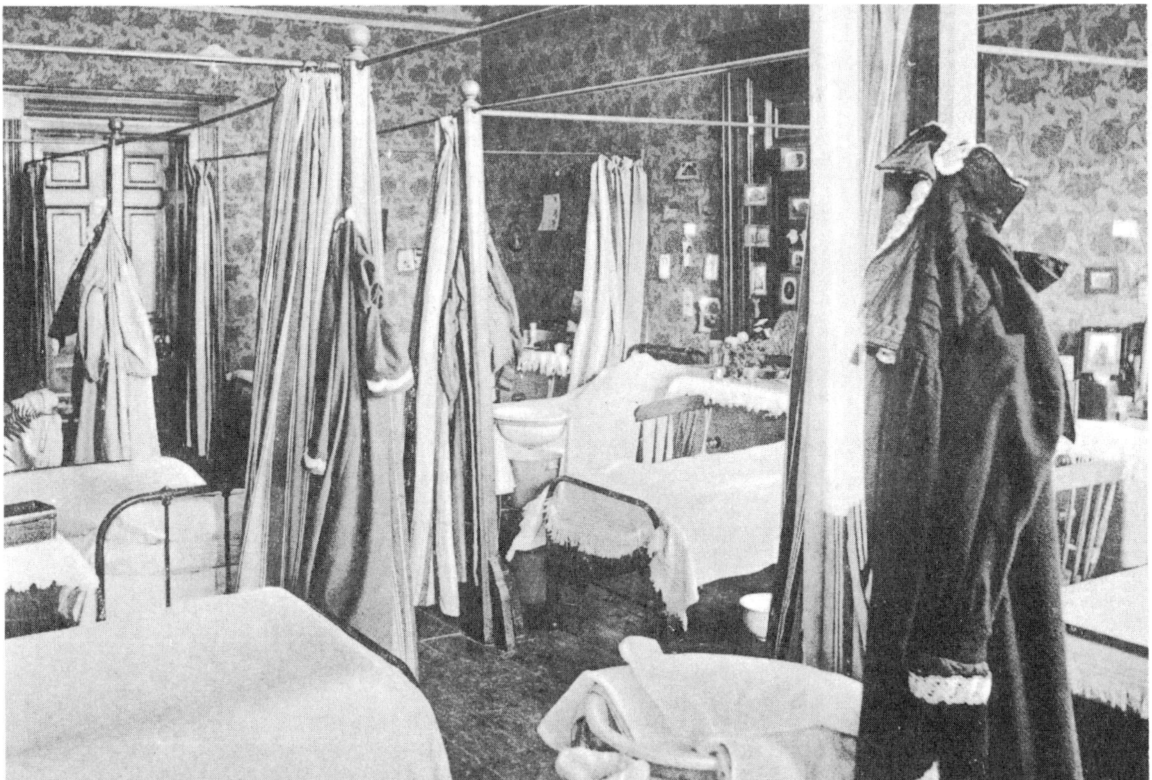

drink water, which was a potential health problem, not surprisingly given Cheltenham's hopeless drainage system. In 1873, 'About 3 am one morning, 40 or 50 [men] students were seized almost simultaneously with purging which went on incessantly till about 10 am.' This was attributed to bad drainage; in reality it must have been food poisoning, which may or may not have been caused by the water. Apart from occasional upsets like this, health at the colleges was surprisingly good. There were few epidemics and only the occasional death.

St Paul's dining room with the famous oak tables

St Mary's dining room in the late 1950s

Although the colleges had expanded somewhat in the 1940s, they were still small enough for the great majority of students to live in college and participate in communal activities. Evening meals were taken together, while students still had to be in college after a set time; at St Mary's this was 10.00 pm on weekdays and 11.00 pm on Saturdays. At St Paul's, the continued existence of dormitories meant that a common 'lights out' time of 10.30 was observed. This close collegiate atmosphere had pros and cons. The great majority of students went to chapel on Sunday. Societies were strongly supported, one reason for this being that they provided an opportunity to meet the opposite sex. Loyalty to their college was taken for granted by most students. At St Mary's rituals which helped to soften the impact of college on first-year students included 'mothers and daughters'. Each second -year 'mother' took a first-year 'daughter' to Brunners, a local tea-room, passing on information about the vagaries of college staff and suchlike. In the early 1950s there were also initiation rites of a fairly harmless nature at St Mary's, in which second-year students dressed up as ghosts. At St Paul's there was still a degree of brutality in the rites, which could involve running a gauntlet of knotted towels while naked. Initiation rites and other 'customs' were not passed down from time immemorial. Their nature and intensity changed quite frequently, depending on factors such as the attitude of staff and the outlook and maturity of students. The more savage aspects of the St Paul's customs seem to have been eradicated in the 1950s.

College discipline remained strict by today's standards; for instance students were not allowed in rooms occupied by the opposite sex. Since the colleges were segregated and a number of staff lived in such rules were easy to police. One result was that after the Saturday night hops (the 1950s equivalent of the disco) couples were wrapped round each other in secluded spots all over the town, including the Park where Winifred Jones would rout them out with the help of her labrador Berry.

St Mary's common room in the late 1960s

This self-contained world started to crumble in the 1960s, although perhaps more of it remained for longer at St Mary's. Far more students now lived out, thus reducing the attraction of college and its activities. Appointed student representatives (proctors at St Paul's) were replaced by elected student councils and student unions affiliated to the National Union of Students. The politicisation of student unions which occurred in the late 1960s and early 1970s seems to have had little impact at St Mary's but at St Paul's the impact included a short-lived strike in 1971. Another change was in dress. In the 1950s college blazers had been an informal uniform for both sexes. From the mid 1960s most St Paul's students adopted the scruffiness which has become the hallmark of the young British male; St Mary's students maintained sartorial standards for longer.

Although the colleges were no longer such cohesive institutions by the 1970s, there were still collective activities which flourished. Many societies in CPM benefited from the increased student numbers of the 1980s. By this time the student union had far greater autonomy than student organisations twenty years earlier so students were forced to take greater responsibility for what were often significant decisions. The unions had merged in 1974, before the colleges; in the 1980s the union promoted women's issues (with the first woman president, Jayne Bolwell, serving from 1982-84) and took a lead in attempts to integrate the growing number of mature students into the structures of the college.

St Paul's common room in the early 1970s

Chapter 5: The Staff

Until the 1890s the staff was small: three or four women and five or six men. Among individual members of staff, Bromby himself was a notable teacher; unlike some training college principals he had taught before, having been Headmaster of Stepney Grammar School. Best known of the college staff in the nineteenth-century was John (Johnny) Gill, the 'Master of Method' (as education lecturers were then called), an ex-bookseller and Methodist preacher. Gill made his career through a natural talent for teaching and a short spell at the Glasgow Normal School, a pioneering training college. He became a headmaster and was then recommended to Cheltenham by an HMI. Gill was a great exponent of the 'object lesson', in which information bearing on all points of the curriculum was drawn out of some everyday object by questioning the children. Although such lessons became something of a joke through their over-use by Victorian teachers, they were in conception a real attempt to relate what was taught to the child's everyday world. Both Gill and Bromby also demonstrated their educational liberalism through their dislike of corporal punishment. Gill was a charismatic though extremely dogmatic educator. His influence was widespread, both through his training of women students (until 1876) and men (until 1888), and through his widely circulated textbooks. The third notable educator in the

Left: *John Gill, master of method 1851-1888*

Right: *Alice Reynolds, lecturer 1887-1918; Lady Superintendent and later Vice-Principal of St Mary's Hall from 1901*

nineteenth century college was Isabella Reynolds. She served between 1849 and 1886, becoming Lady Superintendent of St Mary's Hall in 1864. In some colleges this was simply a pastoral and domestic position, but Reynolds ran both the domestic and academic sides. As early as 1854 an inspector had called her 'one of the most talented women connected with education in this country'. The high reputation of St Mary's throughout the century owes itself partly to her guidance.

As time went by differences between men and women staff, viewed collectively, became evident. Male lecturers often lived out; a student in the 1890s, Frank Tanner, commented that some of these had little connection with the college besides their lecturing. Two exceptions were C H (Charlie) King, the Master of Method from 1887-1912, who carried on the traditions of Gill, and 'Billy' Boone, who taught science and presided over the college's success in London University exams. Boone and King had London external degrees, but they had both been trained at the college as had most of the male staff. The women staff included some old students, such as Lucy Roberts, who pioneered games, the St Mary's magazine and other student activities in the Edwardian period. But there was also an increasing trend towards the appointment of graduates with a postgraduate teaching qualification. There were various reasons for this difference between the women and the men: one was the pressure from old Chelts to appoint male staff from their ranks, a pressure which did not exist in the case of women. Much more than the men, the women formed a close community as they were unmarried, living in at either St Mary's Hall or The Priory.

This pattern continued into the inter-war years, although individual staff changed. Particularly notable among the St Paul's staff were Arthur (Nikki) Mann, who became vice-principal in 1930 and, for his immense loyalty to the college and personal care for students, Reg Riley. Much less remembered is the brief college career of G B Harrison, who taught English between 1922 and 1924; he went on to become a well-known Shakespearean

Left: *Charles King, Master of Method at St Paul's after Gill*

Right: *Miss Cooper, a mistress at St Mary's Hall between 1866 and 1886*

scholar. Beck himself, while a somewhat remote figure, seems to have been respected by students. He was famous for alliteration in speech and writing – an irritating habit to the historian who finds himself unconsciously copying Beck's style. At St Mary's there were a number of exceptional women such as Doris Walker who taught history; Anna Monk, although she seems to have been a caring principal, was overshadowed by Winifred Jones who, as vice-principal and principal, was at the college for thirty years from 1930-60. Emily Brooks, the infant training specialist from 1913-36, should also be mentioned, as she left the money to buy Pallas.

Anna Monk with Priory prefects (senior students) in 1933.

There was probably more participation by staff in the life of the college during the 1950s and 1960s than at any other time, particularly at St Paul's where staff had often been rather aloof in earlier years. In the post-war years staff in both colleges were involved with sport, the students' musical and theatrical activities, societies and the chapel, which up to the 1960s most attended. There was also an active social life. Staff from St Paul's remember the gentlemanly (with a few exceptions) nature of the common room. At St Mary's the staff had a tightly-knit community life little different from the inter-war years: many lived in; they escorted the principal into meals, which all attended; and junior staff had to be prepared to face open criticism from some senior staff in the hierarchical system which prevailed. All this changed in the 1970s and 1980s. Many staff retained an interest in student activities but it became easier to opt out. Common-room life never really developed in CPM with its variety of sites, although gallant attempts were made by the common-room committee.

Edward Bradby with proctors, 1956

A number of staff from both colleges have become known for their literary work. Robert Neill taught biology at St Paul's after the war. With the success of his historical novel *Mist over Pendle* in 1952 he left to take up writing full time. Margaret Greaves (1946-70), who became the head of St Mary's strong English department, wrote a number of children's books such as the novel *The Dagger and the Bird*. Another writer of children's books was Brian Earnshaw, who joined St Paul's in 1965 and left CPM in 1985. Some of the characters in his science fiction are said to be based on staff at St Paul's. Another college author was Leslie Paul, writer-in-residence at CPM between 1981 and 1984. His varied career had included founding the Woodcraft Folk in the 1920s; writing an autobiography, *Angry Young Man*, which launched that phrase on its long career; and producing the Paul Report of 1964 which instigated important changes in the deployment of Church of England clergy. A few years later, in 1988-89, Don Hale, a former student, was writer-in-residence. His plays have won a national reputation; two of them were performed at the Edinburgh Festival by the Drama Society in 1989.

Other staff have been notable within college for the academic and professional leadership which they have provided. There is space here only to name a small number. Many who made major contributions and will be remembered by former students must go unrecorded. At St Paul's John

Priestley was an outstanding figure from 1946-1979, first as head of the PE department and then from 1968 as vice-principal (and twice acting principal). At St Mary's Betty Challinor was head of history from 1945 and then vice-principal from 1962-1976; her organisational skills and care for students found a worthy successor in Dorothy Evans, Vice-Principal of St Mary's and subsequently of CPM until 1988. In subject areas Alan Downes, head of geography 1948-1974 and Harold Sayer, head of art 1948-1976, transformed standards in their respective subjects at St Paul's. Geography was a strong and popular department also at St Mary's under Grace Reeves (1951-73) and subsequently Peter Whiteley. The two colleges' strength in geography was recognised when under John Hancock's leadership the first diversified degree, the BSc in geography and geology, was established. Professional education was obviously a vital study in its own right in a teacher training college. Among those who played an important part were Ron West, who was in charge of primary training at St Paul's from 1954-74, and Alan Mentz at St Mary's and then CPM from 1963 to 1986. The immense task of steering the college's first BEd proposal to CNAA through the then complex validation procedure was handled by Dennis Sutton, who subsequently ran the BEd course at CPM; Gordon Margretts ran the BSc, and Susan O'Brien and then Russell Williams the BA. Two important developments in the 1970s were in-service training run by Jack Shepherd and adult education, latterly organised by Peter Whiteley. Almost at the end of CPM's independent history Peter Easy undertook the successful development of the modular scheme, the linch-pin of the new Cheltenham and Gloucester College's undergraduate programme.

Throughout the college's history the non-teaching staff have played an important part. In the early years at both colleges the housekeeper was a vital figure, as the governors' minutes testify. Among other long-serving staff this century have been 'Sarge' Harper, porter at St Paul's; Alice

'Sarge' Harper, also known as 'My Lord Porter', porter at St Paul's from the 1920s to the 1950s

Cummings and Rose Millward, who retired from St Mary's in 1970 after fifty-one years' service each on the domestic staff; Margaret Thompson, domestic bursar at St Paul's 1951-82; and Brenda Kemeys, now the director's secretary, who has been first at St Paul's and then at CPM since 1959.

Alice Cummings celebrating fifty years on the domestic staff at St Mary's in 1969. (Reproduced by permission of the Gloucestershire Echo)

Chapter 6: Teaching and Learning

After the initial years of experimentation, the syllabus from the 1850s onwards settled down to English grammar, arithmetic and simple factual material in history and geography, with a limited amount of geometry and algebra for the men. Cheltenham, like most colleges, also taught large amounts of divinity. Women did needlework, which was an important subject for girls in elementary schools. In the early years Cheltenham was unusual in that male staff taught the women, though separately from the men, but this faded away in the 1870s. Later in the century the curriculum did broaden somewhat, with science being introduced for the men and French for the women. In English, set poems, plays or novels were read and simple questions about plot or characterisation posed to the students. An 1887 timetable shows that men spent about four hours a week on religious knowledge, six on maths, seven on English and four on science, with small amounts on history and geography. Women spent much the same time on religious knowledge, English and arithmetic (they did not do higher maths), plus three hours a week on needlework and two on French. Timetabled teaching hours came to twenty-six per week for the men, with another twenty hours of private study; and thirty-one and eleven for the women.

The men's practising school, by Aylwin Sampson

As these figures suggest the main method of teaching was lectures; there was only limited opportunity for private reading. To relieve this monotonous course of study there was the practical training, supervised by the Master (and later also the Mistress) of Method. The men's department

The criticism room at St Mary's

had its practising school behind the main college, where students spent several weeks teaching; there was also a 'model' school in the same building, where the students observed but did not teach. St Mary's used local schools for the same purpose. Women and men students also had to undergo 'criticism lessons' – ghastly experiences in which they taught a class of children in specially designed rooms, at the back of which were the other students and staff who subsequently 'criticised' the wretched student concerned. Much later, in the 1940s, when 'crits' were on their last legs, verses were written commemorating one particular unfortunate lesson at St Paul's. A student had rashly decided that the class would construct model caravans out of sugar boxes. Unfortunately he had not provided enough boxes; inviting the boys to help themselves did not improve matters. According to the versifier, the twenty-five boys in the class were 'screaming, fighting, kicking, punching, rolling on the floor . . . ' before the student gave up in despair and ordered them out. Most criticism lessons were not quite so bad as this. Gladys Warden (1910-12) gave a successful one; 'Miss Roberts [the lecturer] told me afterwards it was lovely and she wanted to read it again'.

The advanced chemical laboratory at St Paul's; although this is reproduced from an early twentieth century postcard, the laboratory is said not to have changed much for the next forty years

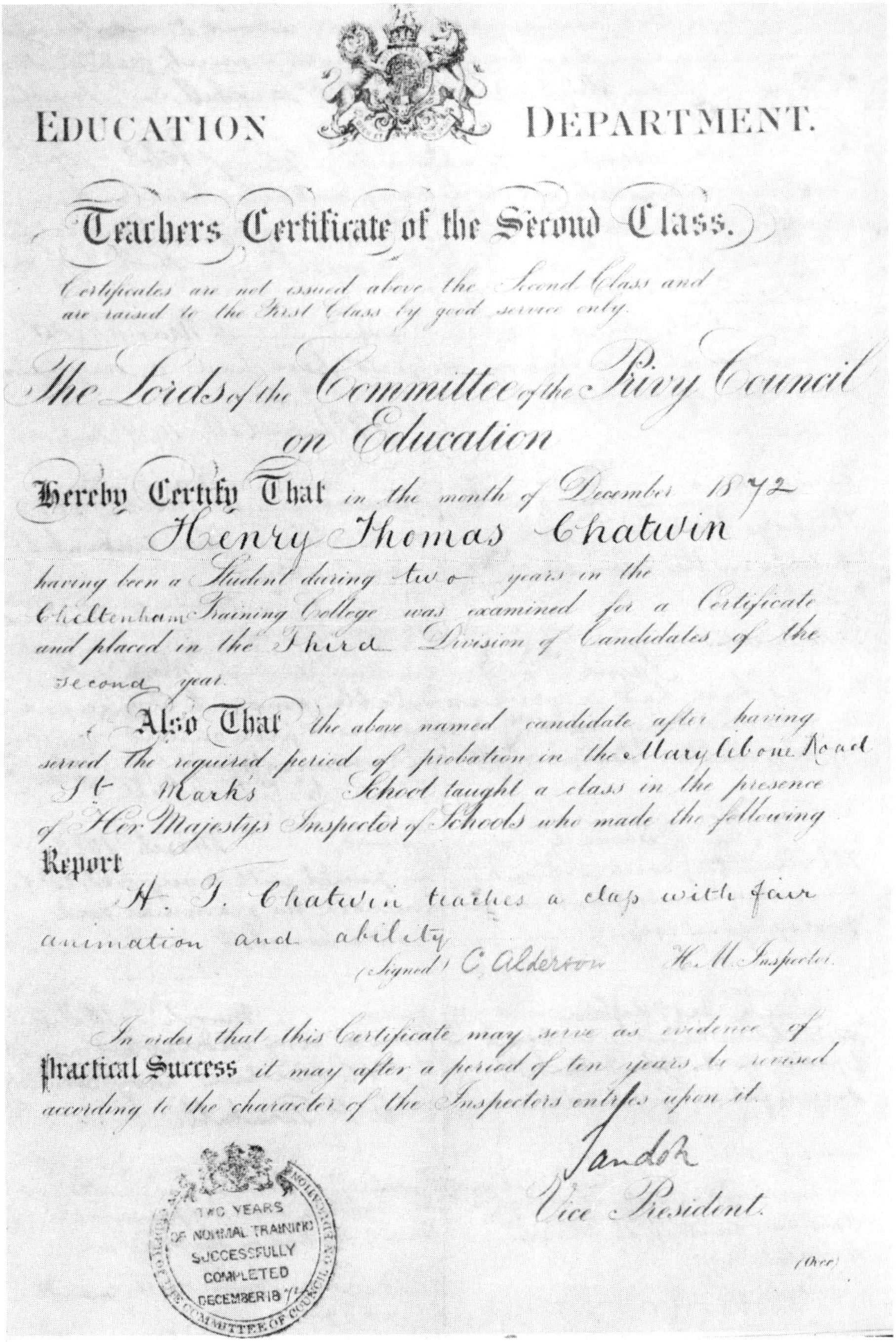
EDUCATION DEPARTMENT.

Teachers Certificate of the Second Class.

Certificates are not issued above the Second Class and are raised to the First Class by good service only.

The Lords of the Committee of the Privy Council on Education

Hereby Certify That in the month of December 1872

Henry Thomas Chatwin

having been a Student during two years in the Cheltenham Training College was examined for a Certificate and placed in the Third Division of Candidates of the second year.

Also That the above named candidate after having served the required period of probation in the Mary lebone Road St Mark's School taught a class in the presence of Her Majesty's Inspector of Schools who made the following

Report

H. T. Chatwin teaches a class with fair animation and ability

(Signed) C. Alderson H. M. Inspector.

In order that this Certificate may serve as evidence of Practical Success it may after a period of ten years be revised according to the character of the Inspectors entries upon it.

Sandon

Vice President.

TWO YEARS OF NORMAL TRAINING SUCCESSFULLY COMPLETED DECEMBER 1872

(Over)

The teacher's certificate of Henry Thomas Chatwin, at St Paul's between 1870 and 1872

In the late nineteenth century new subjects were added, and some students took London University external degrees; the college was particularly noted for its work in science. Bren brought back the use of male staff to teach women, which had faded away earlier. If the lecturer was a bachelor, he had to be accompanied by a female member of staff. If he was married it was thought that he could be safely left by himself. Degree work was given up in the inter-war years, as was the teaching of St Mary's students by St Paul's staff. Students continued to do some work at an advanced level, but still had to take a wide range of other subjects so that they could teach the whole elementary school syllabus if necessary. Women, for instance, had to do cookery, later called domestic economy. Advanced subjects could be of high quality, as history was at St Mary's under Doris Walker and advanced mathematics at St Paul's under D P Smith. Unfortunately other subjects were often not much above the level of school certificate, the standard school-leavers' exam at the time. Practical training was the most valued element of the course for many, with students by now going outside Cheltenham to schools in Gloucester and rural areas.

Rural science at St Mary's in the late 1940s

The persistence of the two-year training courses meant that academic standards in the 1940s remained low compared to today. From the late 1940s an influx of new staff helped to improve the academic level, particularly at St Paul's where standards seem to have fallen during the war years; the shift to coursework assessment also helped by reducing the amount of rote learning. Staff from the period testify to the role of the Bristol University Institute, responsible from 1947 for academic quality, in enhancing standards and providing help and advice. In the 1950s the emphasis was still very much on 'how to teach', and the amount of time allocated to special subjects was inevitably limited by the continued need to spend some time on every subject. Most assignments were much shorter than today's essays, the long studies of a topic of the student's choice being an exception, and the amount of reading expected in individual subjects was less. But a number of subjects reached high levels – geography and art at St Paul's, English at St Mary's, and PE at both colleges, to name only some of the most prominent. Another feature was the ability in a small college to use the timetable flexibly. At St Paul's in the early 1950s lectures were sometimes cancelled in the summer to allow a whole day's break from the grind of lectures. Later there were field weeks, not just for geographers but for other students such as the historians, who managed in 1963 a trip to Moselle and the Rhineland.

In the 1950s students went into both primary and secondary teaching, but from the inception of the three-year course there was a move towards concentration on primary and, at St Paul's, the junior/secondary age range (covering the upper years of primary and lower years of secondary). PE students at both colleges and some other specialists continued to train for the older age group. With the decline in teacher training numbers in the 1970s there was a rapid decline in secondary training outside PE; by the late 1980s it survived only in PE, mathematics and religious education. Training for primary teaching remained an important part of CPM's work and still is important in the new college. For students training for teaching, which meant all students until the 1970s, school experience continued to be an important part of the course as it still is today. Reminiscences suggest that in the 1950s at least criticism of lesson preparation was often tough. With the growth in numbers, students had to go further afield for their experience, to Wiltshire, Oxfordshire and Bristol. Organising school experience and liaising with schools became a major headache for staff. The headmistress in Gloucester who barred college staff from her school if they had not made an appointment may have been exceptional but illustrates the difficulties which could arise.

Within the colleges, there were gradual shifts in teaching style which reflected the greater amount of time available, in particular with the inception of the three-year course in 1960. But as early as 1963 Valentine Hall noted the tendency for subjects to add extra material, limiting the time available for private study. Technology also changed. Language labs were introduced in the mid 1960s and the overhead projector became common. The libraries in both colleges also grew rapidly, although never fast

Left: *Teaching practice, about 1980*

Right: *Teaching practice, about 1980*

enough to keep pace with the numbers of students. St Paul's library was enlarged in the early 1960s; the new St Mary's library at The Park soon had to be enlarged as well. The BSc and BA degrees of the later 1970s and 1980s placed new demands on the libraries, which the librarians strove gallantly to meet with limited resources. The first mention of computers in teaching comes in 1974, when St Mary's established a link with another college's mainframe. By the late 1970s computing was becoming established in geography and geology. In 1985 a substantial investment was made in desktop machines for use with all subjects.

From the beginnings of the honour degree courses there were some gratifying academic successes. Out of five first-class honours degrees awarded for the first time on the Bristol BEd in 1971 three went to St Paul's students. Students from both colleges achieved several more firsts in the 1970s and followed this with similar achievements on the CNAA degrees in the 1980s. For instance, in 1988 there were three firsts on the BEd course and one on the BA; in 1984 two firsts on the BSc, which had a smaller number of students. Standards on degree courses were maintained both by the CNAA's initial validation and by external examiners, many of whom were from universities and polytechnics. Her Majesty's Inspectorate also monitored courses. An inspection report on the BEd in 1983-84 noted that 'the students emerge as individuals with clear views of their own. With few exceptions they work hard and take a serious view of the profession for which they are training'. The report was generally complimentary as was an inspection of the BSc and BA courses in 1984 which noted that 'teaching and learning on both courses are characterised by a strong commitment to the value of good personal relationships and high academic standards'.

Cecil Ballantine with a tutorial group on the BA Combined Studies course discussing English literature in the early 1980s

Chapter 7: Church and Chapel

The college's original trust deed, which still stands, states that 'it is solemnly intended and purposed that the religious education to be conveyed shall always be *strictly Scriptural, Evangelical and Protestant*, and in *strict* accordance with the *Articles and Liturgy* of the Church of England . . . ' In view of this it may seem surprising that the college did not have a chapel. Its absence reflected the college's close relationship with the group of Evangelical parishes in central Cheltenham of which St Mary's was the most senior. Bromby, the first principal, was vicar of St Paul's, another of these parishes. From the college's foundation until the 1900s the men went to St Paul's church on Sundays. (St Paul's church was built 1827-31 and lies to the north-east of the college; it is based on the Temple of Ilissus.) Comments by the principals, and other evidence, suggest that after a brief period in the early years the hold of Anglican Evangelicalism on most male students was not strong. After 1870 students increasingly came from board rather than

The chapel

church schools and could expect to make their career in the non-denominational sector of education. They were influenced more by Robert Chamney's brief evening talks than the dry services at St Paul's. Women students went first to St Paul's church and then, after the new St Mary's Hall was built, to a temporary church on the site of the future St Matthew's and then to St Matthew's itself. The women were, like the men, less and less dependent upon church schools as future employers; nonetheless religion seems to have played a larger part in the life of women students than of men. Isabella Reynolds' intense Christianity may have been one reason for this. In a letter to a leaving student in 1857 she wrote:

> The thing by which you can most rejoice my heart is, that you should show yourself a faithful and devoted servant of your chosen Master, and by the constant exhibition of all Christian graces, make it manifest that you have 'been with Jesus' . . .

There were a number of reasons why the chapel was built in 1909-10. Perhaps the chief one was Bren's view that in a religious and social climate which had changed greatly since Francis Close's day, a chapel could provide a focus for college loyalty as well as being a less obviously denominational place of worship than the local parish church. The chapel quickly fulfilled Bren's aim and played a central part in college life, and the life of many students, for the next fifty years. As women and men were still strictly segregated, they entered the chapel separately but naturally the Sims' walk back from chapel was a chance for Paulites to snatch illicit meetings with them.

The choir outside the chapel: a photograph of 1930. (Reproduced by permission of the Gloucestershire Echo)

In the 1900s also student participation in Bible-reading and discussion classes was increasing. These originally bore the familiar name of Christian Unions (CUs) and were affiliated to what became the Student Christian Movement (SCM). It is significant that the college CUs in the inter-war period remained affiliated to the SCM (and gradually dropped the

A chapel service in the early 1960s

name CU). The SCM was ecumenical rather than evangelical. The college's support for it reflected the weakness of a distinctively conservative Anglican Evangelical position in this period and also the liberal Evangelical views of the principals from Bren onwards.

The great majority of students continued to attend chapel until the early 1960s. The SCM was also active in the early post-war years: in 1946 Winifred Jones wrote in this connection, 'the outlook of the students (is) wider and more serious than a few years ago . . . ' The building of the small chapel in Derwent Hall, at The Park, in 1961 ironically came at a time when attendance at Sunday evensong was beginning to fall. Although a decreasing proportion of students were regular worshippers, the participation of those who remained became in some ways more active and vital. In 1967 a chapel

A service in the Park chapel in the 1980s

council, involving students and staff from both colleges, was set up replacing the previous advisory committee. Services became more varied: in 1964-65 'A student group playing electric guitars and drums accompanied the Geoffrey Beaumont setting of the Communion service once in each term'. This trend continued in the '70s and '80s. Student activism also encompassed Christian activity abroad – for instance in 1984 students worked in the diocese of Montreal and in Morocco. The continuing relevance of the college's Christian foundation was emphasised in 1984 when Ian Brown was appointed as the first chaplain without any teaching responsibilities.

In the late 1940s specifically Evangelical study groups were revived when branches of the Training Colleges Christian Union were established at both colleges, thus reinstating the name 'Christian Union'. For a number of years, the CU and the SCM branches both continued in existence. The two societies sometimes arranged joint meetings where friendly argument could take place. In the late 1960s the CUs at each college could muster fifty or sixty members, but by this time the SCM was struggling and seems not to have survived into the 1970s. In the 1980s, while the CU continued to flourish, a wider spectrum of denominations became represented through, for instance, the Catholic Society.

For many years divinity (as religious studies was usually then called) was taught in part by the principal. In 1945, as a result of changes brought about by the Butler Education Act, divinity was included for the first time as a Western Joint Board subject and divinity departments were established. Subsequent to the change of name to religious studies in 1970, the subject became even more important in the college with the establishment of diversified degrees. Apart from contributing to the BEd for both primary and secondary students, to the BA and latterly to the modular degree, staff in the department supervise doctoral research and have developed two MA courses, in Church, Religion and Society and in the Interpretation and Use of the Old Testament, in co-operation with Trinity Theological College, Bristol. The Religious Education Centre set up in 1987 has developed material for religious education in schools and provides a resource for local schools and churches.

Chapter 8: The Arts

With the rigorous timetable of the college's early years, there was not much opportunity for creative activities. Nevertheless, the men found time for debates and for the production of a manuscript newspaper. Early examples of this do not survive, but it was revived in 1879 as the *Chelt*, later known as the *Manuscript Chelt* to distinguish it from the printed *Chelt* started around 1890. Both magazines included sports reports, articles by individual students on their special interests and activities, and short stories and 'humorous' pieces – the latter written in that arch, semi-facetious style so redolent of the period. As the atmosphere of the college became more liberal in the later nineteenth century, 'Smokers' (informal concerts at which smoking was allowed) given by year groups became popular. By the 1900s proper concerts in the Town Hall, lasting up to four hours, were the norm. After the building of the chapel in 1910, the college choir, one of the few mixed (although carefully regulated) activities added to the opportunities for music-making.

Art in the 1930s: the Chelt *cover, Easter 1937*

Left: *Country dancing at the 1912 St Mary's Hall reunion*

Right: *Gladys Warden in country dance costume, 1912*

Women's activities remained limited until the turn of the century, although in this the college was no different from the other women's training colleges. Literary and artistic skills went into the production of albums as mementoes of the student's time at college. Each student contributed a poem, drawing or some uplifting homily; if all students had albums, as seems likely, the effort spent must have been prodigious. The entries in a surviving album from the early 1880s are all in the students' best copperplate (contrary to what is sometimes thought, everyday Victorian handwriting was often dreadful). The second half of Angelina Cooper's poem, addressed to Clara Rowberry, the album's owner, went:

Life is real, life is earnest;
And the heroine in the strife
Is the one who leaves the future,
Living but the present life.
Lives it truly, nobly, grandly,
Thus prepares for coming fate;
Strives to make her living perfect
Learning to 'labour and to wait'.

Winifred Jones in an unusual guise: a staff 'Persian play' of the early 1930s. (Reproduced by permission of the Gloucestershire Echo)

The note of stern duty struck in this poem seems a fitting prelude to a period when women were to assume an increasing place in public life. Symbolising this more outgoing atmosphere, in 1902 St Mary's started its own magazine, *Echoes from St Mary's*.

The concerts at St Paul's seem to have contained sketches and excerpts from plays, but it was only in the 1900s that full-scale drama developed. St Mary's students, for example, put on *Cranford*. A Shakespearean play was a regular event. The men's productions may have been rather stereotyped. P H Newby's novel *A Step to Silence*, based on life at St Paul's in the 1930s, suggests that the staff got rather tired of watching R C Sherriff's First World War classic *Journey's End* year after year. In the inter-war period both magazines, and particularly the *Chelt*, reached a high standard; the latter contained several articles in 1937-38 by Newby, who in 1969 was to win the first Booker prize.

Twelth Night, St Mary's Hall, c. 1912

The performers of the St Paul's Junior Concert, c. 1913

Music has been both a subject on the curriculum and a recreation since the nineteenth century. From the 1930s, if not earlier, music teaching and the college choir reached a high standard under John Trueman and then George Budge (1945-62) and Merlin Channon (1962-65) at St Paul's. Unfortunately the 1960s 'wing' policy of concentrating high-level provision of certain subjects in specialist colleges was detrimental to Cheltenham in music with Newton Park College becoming the specialist provider in the region, thus reducing the number of musicians coming to St Paul's and St Mary's. Nevertheless musical activity continued to play an important part in the colleges' life. The Opera Group was founded in 1962; every year it and the Music Society have given public performances of several works, from chamber music to Gilbert and Sullivan to musicals. Among a number of old students who have made notable contributions to the musical world at either amateur or professional level have been the late Forbes Robinson (1943-45), a principal bass at the Royal Opera House from 1954, and the composer Elis Pehkonen (1966-67), who subsequently taught at Cirencester School.

The colleges' dramatic activity also expanded rapidly in the 1950s and 1960s. In the early 1950s Edward Bradby discerned 'rather more enterprise in their [the students'] choice of plays' during a year in which the *Cherry Orchard* and *Lady Precious Stream* was performed. In 1964, when *Oedipus Rex, Henry IV, Part 2* and a light revue comprised the bill, the Drama Society was renamed College Theatre. It was now able to use the old St Mary's assembly hall at Shaftesbury Hall, which had been remodelled to make it more suitable as a theatre. In addition, Theatre in Education, run by Jenny Etherington, has produced plays for children since the 1970s. Perhaps the highlight of the colleges' dramatic and musical history came in the 1970s, when there were a series of outstanding productions of plays by Tony Richards, lecturer in drama 1963-85, with music by Keith Harrison, now Director of Music. *The Melody Man, Perseus* and *The Majesty* achieved widespread critical acclaim.

Choir practice with George Budge in the early 1950s

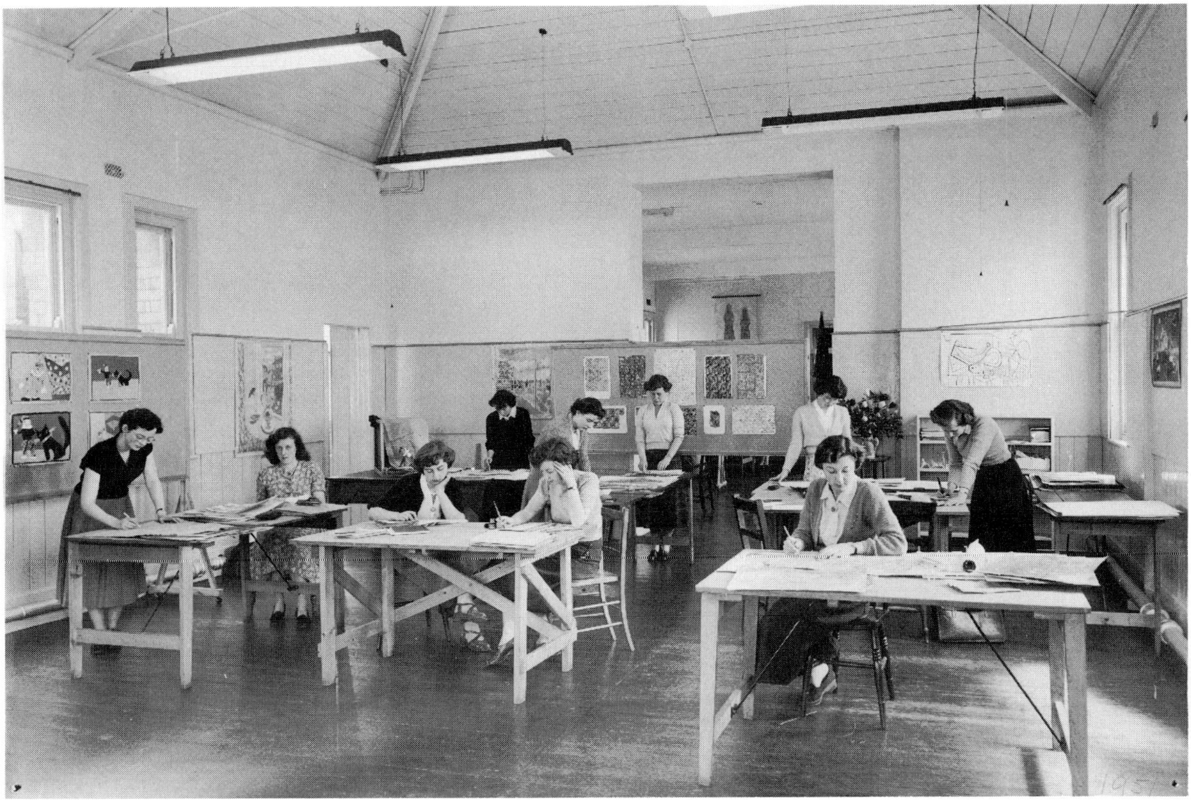

Students at both St Paul's and St Mary's also produced much good work in art and design, at St Paul's under Harold Sayer and Dan Shannon in the department of design, at St Mary's under Joan Adams (1944-72). Shannon, later an HMI, started the Tarsus Press which produced programmes for carol services, plays and the like. Unfortunately in the 1970s national policy led to a reduction in art and design provision at the college –

The craft room at St Mary's in the late 1940s

Left: *'The water carriers': the first woodcut in the St Mary's magazine, 1938*

Right: *Art at St Paul's in the 1960s; the sitter is a Ugandan student*

although with the GlosCat merger the new institution has the infinitely greater resources of the former College of Art. What have been lacking on a regular basis since the end of the 1960s are student magazines. There has been an intermittent Student Union magazine (at one time called *SPASM*, a less polite acronym for the college than CPM) but standards of production were far below the magazines of earlier years. There were also gallant efforts in the 1970s and 1980s to produce poetry magazines, but none of these lasted. The only regular publication in the recent past has been the Rag Magazine, which has plumbed steadily increasing depths of tastlessness.

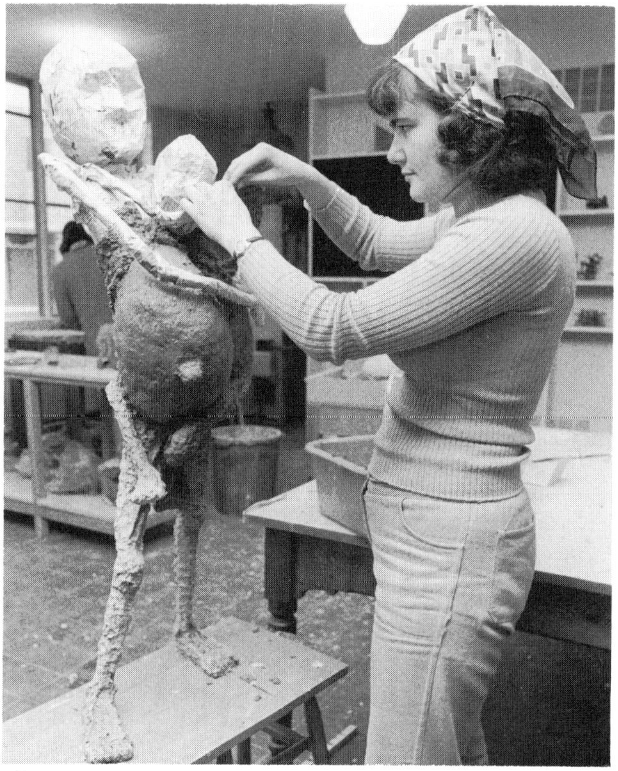

Student with sculpture: 1970s

Chapter 9: Sport and PE

For most of the nineteenth century, anything but the lightest exercise for women was considered unladylike and damaging to health. St Mary's students took virtually no exercise beside the class walks and games of croquet. It was at the men's department that sport developed in the early period. Cricket was played from the 1850s, although it is not clear where. Then in the 1870s Rugby developed in a big way. Cheltenham was a training college pioneer in the game, its growth here occurring only a few years after the game was taken up outside the public schools where it had begun. The dozen or so yearly fixtures in the 1880s included Moseley, one of the oldest Rugby clubs, and local Gloucestershire clubs such as Stroud. By 1889-90 the magazine noted that there were a number of followers of the 'dribbling rules' – a reference to soccer where running with the ball, rather than passing it, was the characteristic tactic at that time. By the 1900s soccer was as important as rugger; the original rented sports ground was replaced by the present grounds in 1904.

Games helped the men forge an *esprit de corps*. The importance attached to them could outweigh most other things: a student writing to support the foundation of a debating society in 1890 lamented pitifully, 'Perhaps some will say that they cannot see how a debating society can be useful here – that it is in fact the reverse because it takes up time which

Cricket at Rosehill

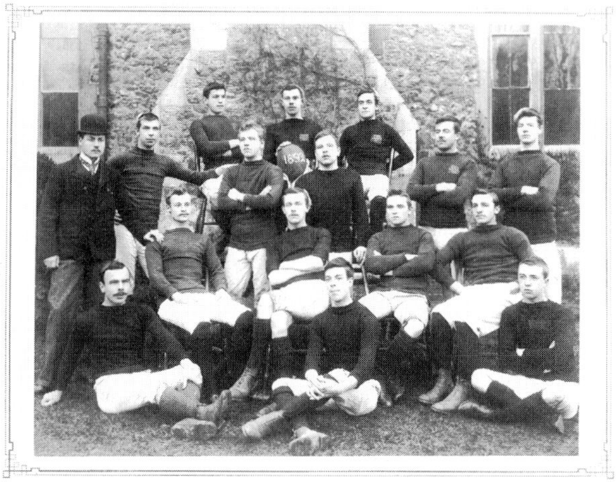

Left: *The cricket XI, 1882*

Right: *The rugby XV, 1891-2 season*

would be better spent in outdoor exercise'. Other sport which the men practised before the First World War included fencing, paper-chasing (a popular sport at that time), water polo which had just begun in 1914, and small-bore rifle shooting in the range – which is still there – constructed beneath the assembly hall.

The tennis net that was bought in 1891 foreshadowed a new era of freedom and activity for women, in sport as in other things. Games-playing, pioneered in girls' public schools, spread quickly to St Mary's. In 1900 a sports field was bought in Old Cemetery Road. (Renamed Market Street; the college disposed of the field, which is still in use as a sports ground, in 1935.) Soon hockey and cricket were being played and a few outside fixtures set up. At much the same time, PE for women developed. In the 1870s St Mary's had introduced callisthenics, light exercise to music which were popular in girls' schools. The students did the exercises in their usual clothing. In 1905 Cecile Heath, who had trained at Southport a specialist PE college became the first PE teacher; she probably used the 'Swedish' or 'Ling' system of progressive training. By now the women wore gym tunics, although they had to wear these underneath their everyday clothes except in the gym itself. Because of the concentration on games, there was less organised provision of PE for men. For a long time, what facilities there were seem not to have been popular. An observant French student, Henri Proix, noted in 1894 that 'since I have been here I have scarcely seen any student on the parallel bars or trapeze'.

St Mary's Hall hockey XI, 1912, with Lucy Roberts

Increasing government concerns about child health led to a growth of PE in schools in the twentieth century. The St Paul's gym was constructed above the rebuilt assembly hall in 1914. In 1937-38 both colleges started advanced PE courses, among the first in the country; St Mary's constructed a new gym at the same time. Games provision in the inter-war years grew as well. St Mary's introduced badminton and netball, while the St Paul's fixture list expanded. By now there were two rugger fifteens and three soccer elevens, each with numerous fixtures. Apart from cricket and tennis, athletics also had regular fixtures. Training colleges, universities and local teams all provided opposition. While sporting provision continued to increase in this period, the big advance had come earlier – for men in the late nineteenth century, for women at the turn of the century.

St Mary's gymnasts in the early 1960s

A PE class at St Paul's in the early 1950s with John Heaton; Gordon Osborn, as a student, is on the right

The advanced PE course which started before the war, although important at the time, did no more than bring PE teaching up to the standard of other subjects. In 1950, however, St Paul's started a third-year supplementary course in PE for promising students as well as serving teachers. St Mary's ran one-term courses for the latter. The expertise thus developed meant that, in 1960, St Paul's and St Mary's were both designated as 'wing' colleges, which meant that they were among the limited number of colleges providing specialist PE courses.

PE training in the early post-war period was highly structured; the emphasis was on how to teach. As time went by the approach changed; PE has become more flexible and students have taken more responsibility. In addition, women's PE has been influenced by the Laban dance movement – as has men's, but to a lesser extent; dance became particularly strong at St Mary's in the 1960s, with the college holding regular dance workshops for schools. PE like all subjects has changed over the years, but throughout both the separate colleges, and later CPM, have maintained a high reputation. Although, as with other subjects, it is somewhat invidious to name individuals, Sheila Aste (1958-78) who became head of PE at St Mary's in 1965 had an outstanding reputation as a choreographer and teacher of dance; at St Paul's, apart from John Priestley, John Heaton (1950-77), who wrote two books on athletics, was one of a number of long-serving staff in the PE department. In recent years Barbara Brown has co-ordinated assistance by PE students with the Special Olympic Games for the disabled.

The strength of PE at the Cheltenham colleges in the post-war years has enhanced their reputation for sport. St Paul's built on its existing Rugby tradition to become a leading college nationally. By the 1960s there were four college fifteens, the first three with over thirty fixtures each per season. The fixture list for the first fifteen included universities such as Cardiff and Bristol, training colleges such as Saltley and Caerleon, and clubs such as Pontypool. In 1978 St Paul's won the British Colleges Cup for the first time, CPM repeating the triumph in 1989. These achievements have been replicated both in other old-established team games and in newer sports. Women's hockey has been a strong sport while the men's hockey team were British Colleges champions three years running between 1979 and 1982. Water-polo has been played at the colleges for many years; the St Paul's team won the national trophy in 1970-71 when Neil Muir, subsequently a member of the British Olympic team, was captain. Some of the numerous other awards include Denise Bradley-Farmer's gold in the British Colleges white-water canoeing in 1982 and the twenty-four medals won by members of the college in the 1989 swimming championship. Other sports at which college students have been consistently successful have included athletics, netball and – a growing sport in the 1980s – trampolining. In the post-war years success in sport helped St Paul's to maintain its name in the teaching community and provided an attraction for students. In more recent years the increasing range of sports and the growth of social sport have catered for the more diversified student community, but not at the expense of the college's position in competitive sport.

A dance class at St Mary's in the early 1970s

Chapter 10: The College in War

In the initial months of World War I, the governors at their regular meetings barely mentioned the conflict. The country's slogan was 'business as usual' and so it seemed was the college's. But soon St Paul's students started to volunteer in large numbers. In some colleges which had territorial companies, practically every student enlisted. Even though Cheltenham did not have such a company, 60 per cent of second-year students had joined up by January 1915. The result of the fall in student numbers was a concentration scheme for the church colleges masterminded by the National Society. The students entering in 1915 went to Chester Training College, accompanied by a Cheltenham lecturer so that they maintained a separate identity, while the second-year men went either to St Peter's Saltley or Battersea. Although no student experience is identical, an example of what might happen to an individual is provided by F A Harrison's wartime career. Coming to college in 1914, he went to Battersea in autumn 1915 but joined up after one term,

Junior year group from the 1914-15 year. F A Harrison is in the front row; C S Clough, H L Greenaway and D D Davies were all killed in the war

serving at first in Malta and subsequently on the Western Front. He then took a degree at Nottingham University on a scheme for ex-servicemen and embarked on a long teaching career at Bablake School, Coventry. In spite of his attenuated training he received a teaching certificate. Between 1916 and 1919 there were no male entries to St Paul's; St Mary's, however, continued with record numbers, taking over the buildings of St Paul's but relinquishing The Priory to the Red Cross. In 1919-1920 the male entry resumed and things got back to normal.

The Second World War was to see more sudden and dramatic change. In the event of war St Mary's Hall had been earmarked for occupation (which never materialised) by a government department evacuated from London. The building had to be vacated and St Mary's moved at short notice to the small Welsh spa of Llandrindod Wells. Winifred Jones and the staff removed all the contents of the college, either to storage or to Llandrindod Wells; equipment was often transported in staff's personal luggage as they made roundabout journeys by train or bus. Three hotels, Bryn-Awel, Baveno, and Lindens, were each used for residence. Bryn-Awel, the largest, had no heating in the bedrooms – and the winter was exceptionally cold. The college returned after four terms, Fullwood now being complete. But the tribulations were not over. On 11 December 1940, as the furniture was being returned, a bomb landed on Fullwood damaging the north wing. Miraculously no one was injured, and although full use of Fullwood had to be delayed another year, St Mary's returned to a semblance of normality. Numbers were high and students led an active social life, as well as indulging in more mundane tasks such as the cultivation of vegetables in the Fullwood grounds.

Bryn-Awel, Llandrindod Wells

That same raid, the largest on Cheltenham, was described by Anthony Baker, a St Paul's student. St Paul's too had been vacated between 1939-40, second-year students going to St John's York and the first-years to either Saltley or Culham. As with St Mary's, the college buildings remained empty and were released in September 1940 when the students returned. The raid started at about 7 p.m. during a history period. While the students were watching a fire at Martyn's, a local factory, from the tower,

> We heard a plane overhead. It began to dive; the whole town was brilliantly illuminated by an orange flare, against which Christ Church Tower was thrown up in sharp relief. The next instant there was a terrific explosion and we all dived for the floor.

The raid went on for three hours, St Paul's, unlike St Mary's, escaping with only broken glass. Just before the raid, in November 1940, the St Paul's College Platoon of the 1st Gloucestershire Battalion Home Guard had been formed with Reg Riley as Commanding Officer. The platoon had various

The aftermath of the Fullwood bomb of 1941

duties over the next few years, including the defence of the town centre in co-operation with the Post Office Platoon. In true Home Guard tradition its initial stock of weapons included twenty pikes. St Paul's continued in operation throughout the Second World War with limited numbers. Vacant space was filled by students from other men's colleges, Culham, Exeter, St Mark and St John, and Chester all being housed in Cheltenham at various times. The latter two used The Priory, which was now surplus to St Mary's requirements.

Cheltenham's roll of honour for each of the World Wars is in the ante-chapel. Ninety-seven former students lost their lives in the Great War, including one St Mary's student who was a VAD. Sixty-three were killed in World War II.

A raid in 1943 resulted in this crater outside St Paul's porter's lodge

Chapter 11: Overseas Links

Samuel Codner, whose letter to Francis Close in 1845 sparked off the idea of the college, had seen it in part as a means of supplying trained teachers to British colonies. In practice, Codner's idea did not materialise in the way that he had anticipated. Hardly any students in the nineteenth century went directly to the colonies from college, although the early old students' handbooks do show that a fair number eventually emigrated, some to teach and others as clergy or missionaries. On the other hand, there were throughout the first forty years occasional trainees from abroad; for instance in 1867-68 A Mercier from Antigua was at the college. Unfortunately when the Siamese legation made enquiries about training in 1891, the college decided that it could not give any help. With considerable farsightedness the Education Department in the 1890s encouraged limited exchanges between English and French colleges. Henri Proix, the French student mentioned in an earlier chapter, presumably came here on one such exchange.

St Paul's students: the 1867-68 year in one of the earliest group photos. Chamney is seated centre; John Gill is to his left; A Mercier is standing third from the left

In the inter-war period financial constraints held back the continuation of exchanges, and it was only after the Second World War that Cheltenham's overseas links developed on a large scale. Edward Bradby worked particularly hard on these links, which involved serving teachers from overseas coming on to the St Paul's courses. For instance in 1953-54 there were seven students from Singapore. Another innovation was a one-year course for overseas students on teaching English as a second language, which ran between 1959 and 1963. One notable overseas student was Omar Arteh, from Somalia, later Somali ambassador to the UN. Subsequently he became a political prisoner in Somalia; past and present students of the college helped in Amnesty International's long and eventually successful campaign for his release. In the late 1950s a St Helenan student came to St Paul's, initiating a continuing link between the island and both colleges. From 1969 onwards college staff regularly visited St Helena while island teachers came to the UK for appropriate training. The 'St Helena Link' at Cheltenham still flourishes in conjunction with several local education authorities. In the 1970s and 1980s the college's involvement with members of the commonwealth became particularly strong when a two-year BEd course was launched for teachers and educators, mainly from Nigeria, who already had a teaching certificate. Financial difficulties led to the course being closed in 1985, but a large number of students had gained degrees in the meantime. Before then, in the late 1970s, there had been a successful certificate course for Rhodesian trainee teachers.

Students on the overseas BEd. on graduation day at Bristol University, 1981. Dorothy Evans is seated centre; Guy Barnes is second on her right

As well as these links with the commonwealth (or in the case of Rhodesia in the 1970s, erstwhile commonwealth), there have also been links with European and American colleges. There were exchanges from the late 1950s between the Cheltenham colleges and French training colleges at Tours and Auteuil; subsequently there have been links with training colleges in Göttingen in Germany and Hamar in Norway, and from 1983 staff-student exchanges have taken place with the Marie-Curie University of Lublin, Poland. From the late 1970s a number of students have regularly come across for six months or a year from the Brethren Colleges, a group of Christian colleges in America. A few students from CPM have made the return journey. The Brethren Colleges link and new links being forged with the help of the ERASMUS programme continue a tradition which has been in existence for well over one hundred years.

Chapter 12: Red-Letter Days

The college's first red-letter day was the laying of the foundation stone by Lord Ashley, later the Earl of Shaftesbury, on the 19 April 1849, a day which a contemporary newspaper described as 'tempestuous and winterly'. The foundation stone itself was oddly worded. It read: 'THIS STONE WAS LAID BY THE RT HONOURABLE LORD ASHLEY MP, PRESIDENT OF THE CHURCH OF ENGLAND TRAINING INSTITUTION. AT CHELTENHAM. FOR THE PURPOSE OF INSTRUCTING PERSONS AS MASTERS . . . ' Only in 1899 were the words 'THIS INSTITUTION WAS FOUNDED' inserted before 'FOR THE PURPOSE', making much better sense.

It was not until 1957 that the college has its first royal visit, when major improvements to St Paul's were inaugurated by the Duke of Edinburgh, who in a morning packed in a chapel service, a tour of the buildings and new kitchens, observations of PE displays and conversations with the cooks and various St Mary's students who were at the ceremonies. Then in 1962 Queen Elizabeth the Queen Mother opened St Mary's new buildings, and in 1987 the Princess Royal opened the primary centre and conferred the degrees at the college's degree ceremony.

The degree ceremony is a quite recent part of the college's history, since there never seems to have been a ceremony to mark the granting of certificates. There were annual Ascension Day services involving the colleges affiliated to the Bristol Institute, which rotated between the cathedrals covering the area served by the colleges. The services are well remembered

Left: *The Queen Mother with senior students at St Mary's*

Right: *The Princess Royal with Janet Trotter*

by those who participated. Degree ceremonies started with the Bristol BEd; until 1977 students and staff travelled down to Bristol for the conferment to be rewarded with strawberries and cream. With the inception of the CNAA degrees the main ceremonies switched to Cheltenham Town Hall where the tea was more modest. In 1984 a graduation ball was inaugurated, to supplement the summer ball. Before the latter was established the custom was to have a valedictory dinner.

The graduation ball is partly an event for former students. It is fitting that this book should end with them. From the first reunion of former students in 1865 there has been a close connection between former students, both women and men, and the college. Former students have contributed to numerous improvements, from the clock on the tower at Francis Close Hall to the library shelving at the Park to the oak tables which once graced the dining hall at St Paul's. Two-and-a-half thousand former students subscribe to the year book. The reunions, once annual and now bi-annual, bring hundreds of former students together. They have constituted important red-letter days for the college for over one hundred years. Over 1,000 former students attended the centenary reunion. Even fifty years earlier, in 1897, the fiftieth anniversary reunion had been attended by 400 'Old Cheltonians, male and female' representing 'five-and-twenty generations of students, many of whom have attained to prominent positions in the educational world'. They included Bishop Bromby, who gave both a speech and a sermon. On being called to give the former he 'advanced to the platform with an elasticity of step remarkable in one who is almost a nonagenarian' (actually he was eighty-three). The present institution, in direct line of succession from Cheltenham Training College, is only five years from its 150th birthday. Will it emulate Bromby's elasticity of step in 1997?

Left: *Betty Challinor, Valentine Hall and Gwen Owen after the Commemoration and Thanksgiving Service in June 1979*

Right: *Canon Hart, Gwen Owen, Marilyn Davies (standing) and Janet Trotter at the Reunion Luncheon, May 1990*